This book is dedicated to the crew of
Mi Amigo

And to the memory of my daughter Kate

Published & Printed by:
ALD Design & Print
279 Sharrow Vale Road
Sheffield S11 8ZF
Great Britain

Telephone 0114 267 9402

ISBN: 1 901587 00 2

First Published 1997, reprinted 2001

Photographs of the crash and unveiling of the memorial stone are courtesy of Sheffield Newspapers. Wartime action shots are courtesy of the United States Air Force.

Cover painting: *Mi Amigo circles at dusk*, by Elizabeth Mottram.

Contents

Acknowledgements

There are many people who have helped, encouraged and contributed, without whom my task would have been impossible.

Bert Cruse of the Royal Air Force Association, who I never had the opportunity to meet, but unknowingly has helped me so much. Arthur Kriegshauser, Pauline Watts and Erma Thompson who have lent me their photographs and have given me an insight of their loved ones. Michael Heath at the American Military Cemetery at Madingley for his help and information. Mike Jackson for taking me, a complete stranger, to the Yorkshire Air Museum at Elvington to see the 8th Air Force historian Roger Freeman. Sheffield Newspapers for access to their archives. Sir David Puttnam for making the excellent movie 'Memphis Belle'. My wife for putting up with losing the dining room for almost four years. And finally, to my father for telling me about the *Mighty Eighth when I was a young boy*.

"The Air Force kind of grew up with the B-17. It was as tough an airplane as was ever built. It was a good honest plane to fly - a pilot's airplane. It did everything we asked it to do, and did it well"
General Curtis E. Le May U.S.A.F.

"The best bomber we had in the war"
General Carl A. Spaatz U.S.A.F

Introduction

For those who know me, my interest in the Mighty Eigth is well-known. The books, pictures and posters that adorn my home and office testify to this. What came as a surprise to me, and many other people living in Sheffield, was the fact that an American World War Two bomber had actually crashed in one of Sheffield's city parks during 1944.

My discovery was quite by chance. I have lived in the Sheffield area since late 1978 but, it wasn't until February 21st 1993, when I was visiting the Imperial War Museum at Duxford, Cambridgeshire, that I stumbled across *Mi Amigo*. I happened to pick up a book by George H. Fox entitled The 8th Air Force Remembered. This excellent book details many of the former airfields and memorials of the U.S. 8th Air Force. On one page reference is made to a memorial stone in Endcliffe Park, Sheffield, marking the spot where ten American airmen died in a B-17 Flying Fortress, *Mi Amigo*.

I was amazed at this revelation as I had visited Endcliffe Park many times in the past with my children and had never seen this memorial stone before. I thought George Fox may have been mistaken. Was it a printing error? How could I have missed such an event? Surely my friends who knew of my interest in the *Mighty Eighth* would have told me.

The next weekend my son James and I visited the park searching for the elusive stone. After some effort we found the memorial. Two simple bronze plaques were mounted on the stone listing the names of the crew. I knew when I found the stone that a full history of the incident should be written.

It has been a long and highly enjoyable task and has taken much longer than I originally anticipated. To all those people who have been patiently waiting for my book, I can only say that I hope it was worth the wait.

Sheffield's Best Kept Secret

I have long described the story of *Mi Amigo* as Sheffield's best kept secret. When I started to investigate the crash I talked to people who had lived in Sheffield throughout the war years. I asked them what they could remember of the incident. Almost everyone who I spoke to looked completely puzzled and thought I had got my wires completely crossed. The mother of a close friend of mine, who has always lived in Sheffield, had no knowledge of the incident and assumed, when I told her of *Mi Amigo,* that the crash must have been the subject of censorship. She could not believe what I was telling her.

As my investigations continued it became increasingly clear that, generally speaking, only those living close to the park during the crash and members of the Royal Air Force Association were aware of *Mi Amigo*. Even those people who had heard of *Mi Amigo* had only a glimmer of the facts. During the years since 1944 details of *Mi Amigo* have got lost and confused. Legends have grown that bear little resemblance to the truth. For many years it was generally believed that she was returning from Germany following a bombing mission.

Mi Amigo was returning from a bombing mission it is true, but from another part of Europe. This goes a long way to explaining why she ended up flying over Sheffield, a fact that has had people curious for many years. Since 1993 I have uncovered much about *Mi Amigo* and her crew. In February 1994 I was fortunate to have collaborated with Yorkshire Television's Edit V programme in the making of a short documentary commemorating the 50th anniversary of *Mi Amigo*. This programme brought to the attention of the inhabitants of Sheffield and South Yorkshire the amazing story of *Mi Amigo*.

Since the documentary was broadcast in 1994 my investigations have continued. I have been extremely fortunate in uncovering information that has remained dormant for fifty years. I have travelled in the U.S.A. on business and uncovered information quite by chance. Many people have tried to investigate *Mi Amigo* but have got no further than old newspaper clippings. On many occasions luck has helped me. Luck has often given me the edge that I needed when I least expected it.

The Mighty Eighth

Following the defeat of France and other allies in the low countries during the summer of 1940, Britain and its empire fought alone against the German Third Reich. The German war machine was highly mechanized and was well prepared for war. When Belgium, Holland and France fell, the Luftwaffe had airbases positioned close to the English Channel. It was only a short flight to bomb British cities, factories, ports and military positions. German bombers would get fighter escorts to and from their targets although it was still a perilous operation. The R.A.F., with its squadrons of Spitfires and Hurricanes, would intercept the German bombers over British territory.

In the two years before the U.S.A. entered the Second World War, R.A.F. Bomber Command embarked on a campaign of bombing targets in Nazi occupied Europe; airfields, factories, railway installations, ports etc. To fly deep into Germany meant that bombers would be at the mercy of flak, deadly and very accurate anti-aircraft guns and hoards of Nazi fighters. Flying to Germany and back would take between four and six hours, depending on the exact target and route taken. R.A.F. fighters only had a limited range taking them just as far as the French and Dutch coasts. From there on, the bombers would have to take care of themselves. As a result, many precious aircrews and aircraft were lost during the daylight raids. The R.A.F. could not sustain these losses and changed its tactics to night operations. The number of aircraft being lost was greatly reduced however, flying at night is always a highly dangerous task with the chance of collision. Also, it could never be certain whether the bombs had been correctly dropped on target in the darkness.

When the Japanese attacked Pearl Harbor on December 7th 1941 Roosevelt and Churchill decided that the defeat of Germany would be paramount before the final defeat of Japan. General Ira Eaker, U.S.A.A.F., had spent time with the R.A.F. observing tactics and practices carried out against Germany in the months leading up to December 1941. Eaker was to command the newly formed 8th Air Force.

He knew that the R.A.F. had suffered high losses during daylight bombing, but believed that if the 8th Air Force bombed by day and the R.A.F. bombed by night, the Germans would find themselves under constant attack. Bomber Command agreed and 'round-the-clock' bombing commenced in 1942.

Eaker believed that the American B-17 Flying Fortress and the B-24 Liberator bombers, flying in tight formations at high altitudes with their heavy .50 calibre machine guns, would produce a defensive rain of fire and fend off any German fighters that may try to attack.

Right:
Typical B-17 bombing formation

Below:
Flak takes off a B-17's wing

However, this was not the case. German 88mm anti-aircraft guns were extremely accurate and claimed more American bombers than the fighters of the Luftwaffe.

Although this close up of battle damage was in the possession of a relative of one of Mi Amigo's crew it is, in fact, another B-17. Maybe Sgt. G Malcolm Williams flew with this aircraft before Mi Amigo was assigned to the 305th Bomb Group.

The German defences could detect bombers massing over England as their radar was far more effective than many people in the past had realized. The Germans would plot and calculate the course of the American bombers and alert their fighter air bases of the impending invasion. The American bombers would never fly a direct route to their target, but fly a *'dog's hind leg'* course hoping to confuse and confound the enemy. However, the flak and fighters were always waiting and the casualties were horrendous.

Emblem of the Eighth Air Force

The 305th Bomb Group

The *Mighty Eighth,* when it arrived in Britain, was to occupy about 120 airfields, most of which were in the east of England in an area known as East Anglia. The topography for this area is extremely flat making it perfect for airfields. It is also very close to the English Channel and the North Sea, therefore, ideal for operations. Each airfield was known as a group and each group would normally be made up of four squadrons. Just east of Northampton is the town of Higham Ferrers and nearby is the village of Chelveston. Chelveston is a small farming area with a small community and an ancient Norman church. In 1939 the R.A.F. contracted Taylor Woodrow Ltd to build a new airfield.

In 1942 the 305th Bomb Group arrived under the command of Colonel Curtis Le May. Le May was an excellent tactition and leader of men. His reputation was well-known not only by his own men, but also the U.S.A.A.F. officialdom. Le May was not a great lover of *red-tape.* He knew his job was to train young aircrews ready for combat. Having to deal with huge amounts of incomprehensible paperwork when trying to fight a war was, at times, beyond Le May's patience. His nickname was to become *'Iron Ass'*, a name that was to stick. Le May was an experienced pilot. He developed many new daylight bombing strategies which would very quickly become standard practice for the *Mighty Eighth.*

The sleepy village of Chelveston consisted of a few dozen families. Almost overnight its population was swollen by the influx of three thousand American airmen of the U.S.A.A.F. Most of these men would be ground crew servicing and maintaining the Flying Fortress bombers. The tiny roads around Chelveston would have been grossly inadequate for the large numbers of Dodge vehicles with their constant stream of supplies that would be needed to keep aircraft flying and men fed. Many of the local families would benefit financially from the arrival of the *Yanks,* taking in laundry, supplying fresh vegetables, eggs, etc.

The nearby pubs, The Swan and The Chequers, were favourite haunts for the airmen and, to this day, there are reminders in these pubs of their former American customers.

The 305th was a highly developed Bomb Group and its successes under the leadership of Curtis Le May soon became established. The 305th had its own crest, a steel winged gauntlet holding a bomb and smashing a swastika. Above the crest was the group's motto '*CAN DO'*. These two simple words exemplified the 305th Bomb Group. The 305th had four squadrons; the 364th, 365th, 366th and the 422nd.

364th Bomb Squadron

305th Bomb Group

In May 1943 a raid was made on Schweinfurt, Germany. The target was a ball-bearing factory. Much of the German armaments depended on ball-bearings. Without these small but simple items tanks, trucks, ships and aircraft would be unable to operate. It was believed that by knocking out this one factory serious disruption would be brought to the Third Reich's war effort. The raid was made up of dozens of Flying Fortresses from many different groups, including the 305th. The toll was extremely heavy with many aircraft and crews being lost. Within weeks of the raid the factory was back in production. As the months went by it was realized, by Bomber Command, that another raid would be necessary to knock out the plant. So, once again, massed formations of Flying Fortresses of the *Mighty Eighth* were assembled. The 305th contributed eighteen of its Flying Fortresses for the raid. Shortly after take-off three aircraft had to return to Chelveston with mechanical failures. The remaining fifteen Flying Fortresses formed up with aircraft from other groups. When the formations were complete they set their course for Schweinfurt.

The German radar defences were able to detect the massing bombers early on and soon plotted their course and objective as Schweinfurt. The flak and Luftwaffe were ready for the American bombers and very quickly started to destroy the Flying Fortresses. The losses that day were terrible. A total of sixty American bombers were lost along with six hundred airmen. Of the fifteen aircraft from the 305th only two would return to England. It was the highest percentage loss that any group would suffer during World War Two. This day would become infamous in air warfare. It became known as Black Thursday. The date was October 14th 1943.

B-17G Flying Fortress Mi Amigo

October 14th 1943, Seattle, Washington, U.S.A. Another B-17G Flying Fortress rolled off the production line at the Boeing aircraft factory. This particular aircraft serial number was 42/31322 and when delivered to its new crew would become *Mi Amigo*. The B-17 Flying Fortress is arguably the most beautiful of all World War Two bombers ever built. No other aircraft looks like it with its superb lines and sweeping curves.

The Flying Fortress was first produced in 1935 and over the next ten years would go through many changes. The first Flying Fortresses to see action were the B-17C version which flew with the R.A.F. They were not a success and were found to be lacking in defensive armament. Back at Boeing, the aircraft was given a new tail section with a rear gunner's position and a remote controlled turret underneath the fuselage. This new design became the B-17E. Further developments took place, most notably, the remote controlled turret beneath the fuselage being replaced by a manned ball turret. The ball turret was extremely small and a man of small stature was required to operate this position. This Fortress became the B-17F, but following combat experience, especially the disasterous Schweinfurt raid, it showed that further armament was required and so the last version, the B-17G, was born. With the B-17G model the aircraft really lived up to its name, bristling with a total of thirteen .50 calibre machine guns. Most notably on the G variant the aircraft sported a chin turret which was operated by the bombardier.

The B-17G was one of the most heavily armed bombers of World War Two. It had a crew of ten; pilot, co-pilot, navigator, bombardier, radio operator, top turret/engineer, two waist gunners, ball-turret gunner and tail gunner. The bomb load normally consisted of ten 500lb general purpose bombs stacked vertically behind the top-turret position and in front of the radio operator's cabin.

Four Wright Cyclone radial engines powered the B-17. The engines were equipped with turbo-chargers which enabled the aircraft to fly at higher altitudes. The very accurate Norden computing bombsight was positioned in the perspex nose of the aircraft. Just behind this position the navigator sat at his small table plotting and constantly checking the course. All the crew, with the exception of the pilot and co-pilot, would operate the .50 calibre guns during an attack by enemy fighters. The 'kills' being indicated with German crosses on the nose of the B-17 alongside the mission markers, which would normally be shown by a bomb symbol.

During 1943, crews completing twenty-five missions would return home to the U.S.A. In reality, the average number of missions that the crews made would only number fifteen. It was then that their 'luck' would run out. As conditions improved during 1944 and early 1945 the number of missions was increased to thirty-five.

It was very common for the crews to give their aircraft a name and to add the distinctive nose-art, usually depicting a very suggestive female form. Unfortunately, there is no record as to whether *Mi Amigo* ever possessed any nose-art.

When B-17G serial number 42/31322 rolled off the Boeing production plant at Seattle on October 14th 1943, she wasn't altogether complete. Guns, radio, bombsights, etc. still needed to be fitted and for the next few weeks 42/31322 was flown around the U.S.A. having various pieces of equipment installed.

Details of 42/31322 progress in the weeks following its departure from Seattle are shown below;

Depart Boeing, Seattle, Washington	October 14th 1943
Vandalia, Airbase, Illinois	November 29th 1943
Des Moines, Illinois	December 1st 1943
Denver, Colorado	December 2nd 1943
Cheyenne, Wyoming	December 11th 1943
Kearney, Nebraska	December 22nd 1943
Assigned to E.T.O.	
[European Theatre of Operations]	January 11th 1944
Arrived Prestwick, Scotland	January 16th 1944
Chelveston, Northamptonshire	January 30th 1944

In mid January 1944, 42/31322 was flown to Great Britain taking the northerly route via Newfoundland, Greenland, Iceland and finally touching down in Prestwick, Scotland. On January 30th 1944, 42/31322 was supplied as one of a batch of three replacement B-17Gs to the 305th Bomb Group at Chelveston. She was assigned to the 364th Bomb Squadron. The squadron identification code for the aircraft WF-V being clearly displayed on both sides of the fuselage. A large white letter G in a black triangle was painted on both sides of the large tail. This G indicated that this aircraft came from the 305th Bomb Group.

The crew of 42/31322 had arrived earlier in November and they would have flown as spare crew for other bombers until they were assigned their own aircraft. However, as of January 30th, the crew finally had their own B-17.

The name *Mi Amigo*, meaning *my friend* was suggested by Lt. Melchor Hernandez, the bombardier. He was of Spanish extraction and the name *Mi Amigo* reflected the admiration he had for the B-17. The name was readily agreed by the crew. American air crews often named their aircraft in just the same way that ancient mariners had given names to their ships down through the centuries. The name represented a talisman, a goodluck charm. The crews would need all the luck they could get. When crews chose the names for their aircraft it was common that the same name would be used on many other aircraft. However, *Mi Amigo* was totally unique.

Boeing B-17G Flying Fortress Specification

Aircraft type : 10 man long range medium bomber
Powerplant : 4 x 1,200 horse power turbocharged
Wright Cyclone radial piston engines
Performance : Maximum speed 287 m.p.h. at 25,000 ft
cruising speed 182 m.p.h.
service ceiling 35,800 ft
Dimensions : Wing span 103ft 9in
Overall length 74ft 4in
height : 19ft 1in
Armament : 13 x .50 calibre machine guns
Bomb load 4,000lbs - long range

The Legend that is The Flying Fortress

The Boeing B-17 Flying Fortress has become legendary in the history of aviation. It was loved by its crews and widely believed to be more rugged than its contemporary, the B-24 Liberator. The Flying Fortress was well-known for taking unbelievable amounts of damage from enemy gun fire and, with wings torn and tail shredded, this amazing aircraft still got its crews home.

Legend became even stronger, particularly with the release of the now famous documentary 'Memphis Belle'. This short colour film was made by the Hollywood film director William Wyler. It was filmed in actual combat conditions over the skies of Europe using hand held 16mm cameras and documented the first B-17 to complete twenty five-missions. The film was released in 1944 and was a huge success with audiences. It is still considered today to be the finest of all World War Two documentaries.

In 1989 Sir David Puttnam produced the movie 'Memphis Belle'. Interestingly, the film is co-produced by Catherine Wyler, the daughter of William Wyler who made the original war time documentary. This was not a remake of the original, but a fictional account of a crew trying desperately to complete its twenty-five missions. Five ageing Flying Fortresses were assembled in England and filming commenced at R.A.F. Binbrook in Lincolnshire. The film portrays many events that occurred to Flying Fortresses, but does not try to glamorize war. It well illustrates the ordeals of all allied airmen who risked their all.

There are several flying examples of B-17 Flying Fortresses still to be seen. Here in Britain, B-17G *Sally B* is a regular performer at air shows and is a worthy example of an aircraft that was once a very common site in the skies of southern England.

The Crew

The crew of *Mi Amigo* came from the length and breadth of the United States. Ten young men who had been thrown together were to participate in the largest aerial bombing campaign known to mankind. The crew had trained for many months, and in some cases years, before they were finally brought together as a complete crew. They were assembled at Geiger Field, Spokane, Washington. There they would practice all that they had been taught during their many months of training, but nothing would or could prepare them for what was to come.

Mi Amigo's crew consisted of ten men;

1st Lt. John G Kriegshauser	Pilot
2nd Lt. Lyle J Curtis	Co-Pilot
2nd Lt. Melchor Hernandez	Bombardier
2nd Lt. John Humphrey	Navigator
Sgt. Charles Tuttle	Ball-Turret Gunner
Sgt. Harry Estabrooks	Engineer/Top Turret Gunner
S/Sgt. Robert E Mayfield	Radio Operator
Sgt. Vito Ambrosio	Right Waist Gunner
M/Sgt. George M. Williams	Left Waist Gunner
Sgt. Maurice O Robbins	Tail Gunner

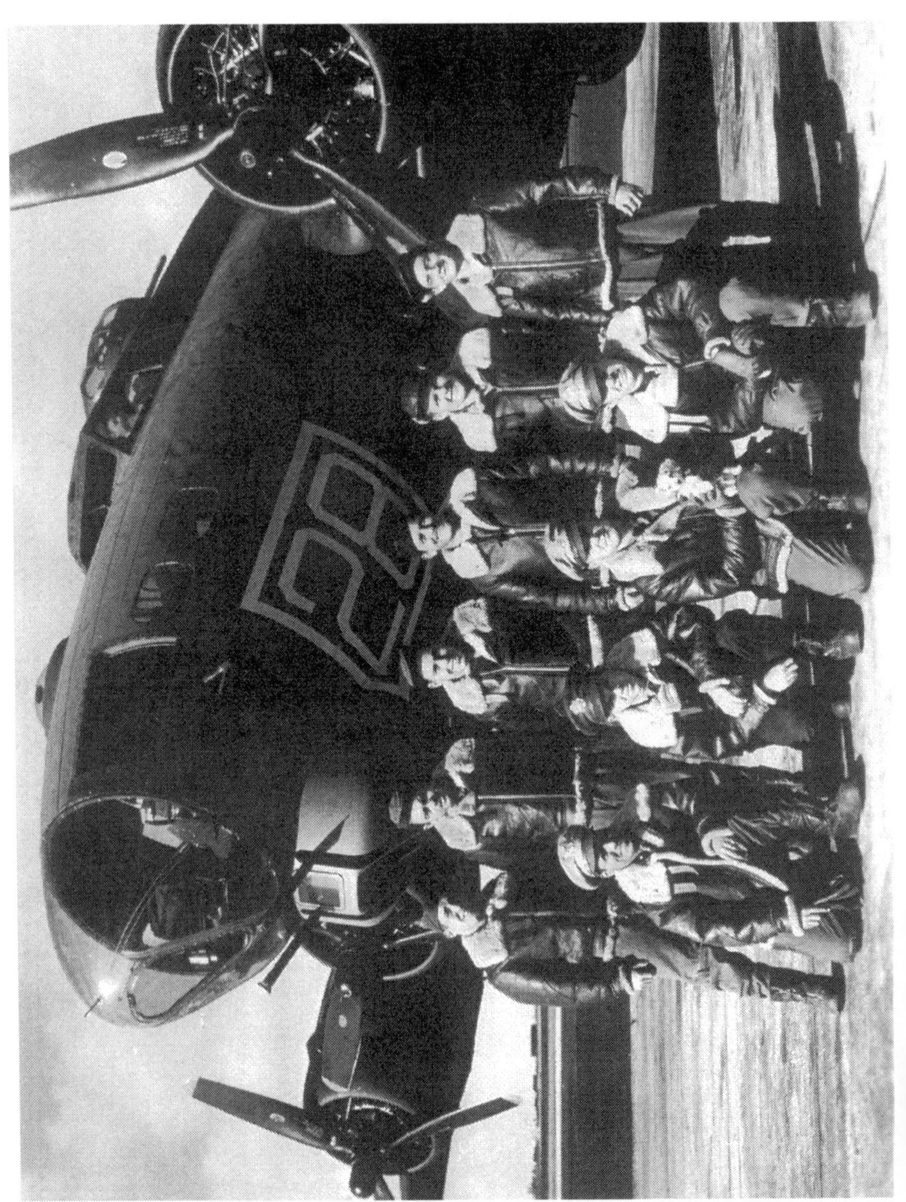

LEFT-RIGHT REAR			
S/SGT	ESTABROCK	ENGINEER	(KAN)
SGT	ROBBINS	TAIL-GUNNER	(TEX)
S/SGT	MAYFIELD	RADIO OPERATOR	(ILL)
SGT	AMBROSIO	ENGINEER	(NY)
SGT	TUTTLE	BALL TURRET-GUNNER	(KEN)
SGT	WILLIAMS	WAIST-GUNNER	(OKLA)

FRONT ROW			
LT	HERNANDEZ	BOMBADIER	(CALIF)
LT	HUMPHREY	NAVIGATOR	(ILL)
LT	CURTIS	CO-PILOT	(WYO)
LT	KRIEGSHAUSER	PILOT	(MO)
MASCOT-"PEANUTS"		NUISANCE	???

GEIGER FIELD- SPOKANE WASH - OCTOBER - 22 - 1943

Handwritten notes on the reverse of the group photo, note remarks for Peanuts. This photo was taken while the crew were training in America. The aircraft is not Mi Amigo, but in fact another B-17G named Shebolli.

1st Lt. John Glennon Kriegshauser, Pilot

John Kriegshauser was born in St. Louis, Missouri, July 2nd 1920. He came from a middle class background of German descent. John graduated from the Roosevelt High School in St. Louis and started work in the warehouse at the Continental Shoe factory. He enjoyed playing softball with his brother Arthur and friends, but one of his real loves was his 1936 Ford Sedan. During his time at the Continental Shoe Factory John bought himself a short wave radio.

This eventually led him to join the Army Air Corps on August 8th 1940. He became an instructor of radio and achieved the rank of sergeant.

Later, when the U.S.A. became involved in World War Two, John was selected for pilot training, achieving the rank of Lieutenant. Before leaving the United States John became engaged to a girl named Peg from Columbus, Ohio.

During his time with the 305th Bomb Group John flew a total of fifteen missions.

Above and Below: John Kriegshauser with his 1936 Ford Sedan

In 1945, following John's death, the Distinguished Flying Cross medal was posthumously awarded. The D.F.C. and the Air Medal with oakleaf cluster were presented to his parents on January 24th 1945 at a ceremony at Scott Field.

The citation for the D.F.C. stated;

"Displaying consummate skill, he piloted the aircraft back to England. Although weather conditions were prevalent Lt. Kriegshauser attempted to locate a field in which to land. Engines became inoperative over a heavily built up area and he was forced to crash land. An English home was directly in the path of the bomber, but Lt. Kriegshauser, exhibiting an exemplary devotion to duty, manoeuvred the crippled aeroplane over the dwelling. It crashed approximately 100 yards away. The courage, coolness and skill displayed by Lt. Kriegshauser, reflect the highest credit on himself and the armed forces of the United States of America"

Ar and Mrs Kriegshauser eceiving the D.F.C. & Air Medal

The Purple Heart was received by John's parents March 23rd 1945.

2nd Lt. Lyle J Curtis, Co-Pilot

Lyle Curtis was born March 27th 1921 at Wrigg, approximately fifty miles from the city of Idaho Falls, Idaho. Lyle never knew his mother, as she died within days of his birth.

Lyle lived with his father on a farm raising horses. He went to Grade School at Wrigg and attended High School at Ucon where he and his father settled. The area in which they lived was a Mormon farming community and Lyle regularly attended the local Mormon church. This is where he met his future wife, Erma.

Lyle was popular with his friends and, like John Kriegshauser, was fond of ball games. He was also very interested in raising horses and intended that, after the war had finished, he would have his own farm and raise horses as his father had done.

Lyle joined the Army Air Corps on December 30th 1941, just three weeks after Pearl Harbor. He decided to join the Air Corps rather than get drafted into the Army. During Lyle's training he developed measles and was so badly affected by it that he was almost retired. The disease put Lyle's training back by many months. During a ten day leave in 1943 he married his eighteen year old sweetheart, Erma, at the Mormon Tabernacle Temple, at Salt Lake City, Utah.

Erma & Lyle outside the Mormon Tabernacle Temple on their wedding day

Peanuts the dog

Lyle was, at this time, based at Geiger Field, Washington. He lived with his wife in a hotel just off the air base for just six weeks before he was posted to England with his fellow crew members. Before Lyle left the United States he bought a little dog which he called Peanuts. Lyle's wife, Erma, thought the dog was a present for her, to keep her company when Lyle would be posted away.

Lyle explained to her that the dog was to be the crew's mascot and was going to England with them. In the crew photograph at Geiger Field Lyle can be seen proudly holding Peanuts. What became of Peanuts nobody knows.

Whilst Lyle was at Chelveston he found himself quite lonely, as do so many servicemen away from their homes and their families. One Sunday Lyle made his way into Higham Ferrers. He stopped a passer-by hoping to get directions to a Mormon church. The passer-by explained that there were no Mormon churches in the town. However, they were going to the local Methodist church and invited Lyle to accompany them. He gladly accepted. Lyle was invited home following the church service and was warmly received by the Lynne family. They had sons away overseas in the services and treated Lyle as if he was one of their own. This was not uncommon during the war. Many families would take in young servicemen away from home hoping that maybe someone would do the same for their sons, wherever they may be.

When Lyle was at Chelveston he received news that he was to become a father. News which greatly excited him but, unfortunately, he was never to see his daughter born.

2nd Lt. John W Humphrey, Navigator

John Humphrey was born July 17th 1920 in Wyoming, Illinois. Little is known about John other than that he was a devout Catholic and that he had two ambitions which he was to realize. One was to fly and the other to visit Europe. John graduated from the Wyoming High School in 1937. He then attended the Knox College, Galesberg, Illinois for two years. On January 2nd 1943 John enlisted into the Air Corps. He received his navigators' wings at San Marcos, Texas August 7th 1943. As navigator, John was responsible for ensuring that the pilots were given the correct course to fly, constantly checking and rechecking the position of the aircraft. Before each mission great detail would be given during briefings. Huge maps and charts would hang from the interiors of the Briefing Room. Details of the course to be taken were minutely explained along with likely flak emplacements to try and avoid. Secondary targets were always a possibility because of bad weather so careful notes about the weather forecasts would be meticulously made.

There would always be a lead aircraft in a group with its navigator plotting the course. However, the lead aircraft would often get shot down, so it was always possible that any of the other aircraft would be called to become the lead aircraft. The navigator's job was a demanding position. During an attack by enemy fighters he would have to wear a flak jacket and steel helmet, whilst manning a .50 calibre machine gun in the confined nose section, alongside the bombardier.

2nd Lt. Melchor Hernandez, Bombardier

Melchor Hernandez came from Los Angeles, California and was born of Spanish extraction. Little is known about Melchor, but it is certain that Melchor gave their aircraft the name *Mi Amigo.* As bombardier it was his job to ensure that the bombs were dropped on target. The B-17G had the Norden bombsight which, in 1944, was considered the most advanced bombsight available. When on a bomb run, the bombardier would be flying the aircraft from his bent up position over the bombsight in the perspex nose of the aircraft. Unlike the earlier B-17s, the B-17G had the remotely controlled chin-turret, with twin .50 calibre machine guns, which were operated by the bombardier. The purpose of this added defence was to ward off, or shoot down, the fighters of the Luftwaffe with their famous deadly head-on attacks.

S/Sgt. Harry W Estabrooks, Engineer/Top-Turret Gunner

Harry Estabrooks was born in 1922 and came from the small community of Mound Valley, Kansas. When Harry was young his mother died and he was brought up by his uncle and aunt who cared for him as though he was their own son. Harry graduated from the Mound Valley High School in 1941. When Harry went to join the army he was haunted by a great fear that he would not pass the rigid physical examination, as he was slight of build.

When he did pass the physical he was afraid the war would be over before he could complete his training and get 'over there' but he advanced rapidly.

As flight engineer Harry had to know every nut and bolt of the aircraft. During normal flight he would monitor and assist the pilot and co-pilot in their duties, especially during take off and landing. When the aircraft was likely to come under attack he would man the electrically operated top turret gun position with its twin .50 calibre machine guns. Of all the gunners' positions, this offered the best all round view.

Sgt. Charles H Tuttle, Ball Turret Gunner

Charles Tuttle was born in 1923 and came from the small town of Raceland, Kentucky. He lived with his mother, father and sister Frances. Charles attended the Raceland High School overlooking the nearby railway sidings which, during early 1942, saw many huge troop trains massing. According to his English teacher, Edna Lang, Charles would watch and wave to the passing G.I.s. Many of the teenagers, as a result, would join up with one of the armed services and so it was with Charles.

Above: Raceland High School. Below: Memorial plaque today mounted in Tuttle's home town

Charles enlisted in the Air Corps on October 18th 1942 at Portsmouth, Ohio. To man the ball turret required a person small enough to squeeze into the small sphere, with its two .50 calibre guns. It was an extremely lonely position with little visibility and entirely cut off from the rest of the crew. The idea of the ball turret was to offer protection to the underside of the aircraft from attacking fighters. The gunner inside the ball turret had an extremely vulnerable position. It was not for the claustrophobic.

S/Sgt. Robert E Mayfield, Radio Operator

Robert Mayfield was born on September 29th 1922 in Raymond, Illinois. As radio operator Robert would monitor all radio communications from operational H.Q. and any intercepts from other aircraft. It was normal practice, however, not to communicate with the B-17s by radio leading up to the target. It was known that the German defences would be monitoring the airwaves hoping to glean information of the size and destination of the massed formations of aircraft. In the radio compartment Robert would have a single .50 calibre machine gun which was mounted at the top of the fuselage looking back towards the tail.

Sgt. Vito R Ambrosio, Right Waist Gunner

Vito Ambrosio was born on September 2nd 1919 and was of Italian descent. Vito and his family lived in Brooklyn, New York. Not much is known about him except that he was married the day before he left for England. Vito was one of two waist gunners who were positioned two thirds of the way down the fuselage. Vito would have stood for most of the flight to and from the target, constantly scanning the skies for enemy aircraft. He would have manned his single .50 calibre machine gun ready to fire at any attacking fighters.

M/Sgt. George Malcolm Williams, Left Waist Gunner

George Malcolm Williams was born on December 2nd 1920 at Junction City, Oklahoma. Although named George, he was known to his family and friends as Malcolm however, he had the nickname of 'Pert'. Malcolm lived with his parents, four sisters and two brothers in the town of Faxon, Oklahoma. As a student Malcolm attended the Geronimo High School until his eleventh year and then went to Tankowa and enrolled in the N.Y.A. school where he studied radio. He stayed there for six months before returning to Geronimo.

Malcolm poses with his guitar

Malcolm is said to have had a 'grand personality' with a good sense of humour amusing his friends with jokes and stories. He was musically inclined and, with a friend, they had their own band playing at school halls and local dances. Malcolm played guitar and sang in the band. With his band he made a few records and also performed on KSWO radio. A regular request from audiences was for Malcolm to perform Stardust, which just happened to be his favourite song. On November 18th 1942 Malcolm enlisted into the Air Corps. He went to Oklahoma City for his physical, passed and was eventually despatched to Sheppard Field, Wichita Falls, Texas for training.

Further periods of instruction took place at Boeing Air Field where Malcolm was promoted to corporal and later attained the rank of sergeant at Geiger Field, Washington. In November 1943 Malcolm received his orders to go overseas. He was granted a few days leave to return home and visit his family before sailing for England. With his family around him he told his mother *"Mama, I'll be back, Mama I'll be back"*. To this day the phrase has long been remembered by his family.

As with Vito Ambrosio, Malcolm would have spent many hours huddled over his machine gun. At the high altitude they were flying, conditions were freezing. The gunners were dressed in leather flying jackets and trousers lined with sheepskin. Beneath this they would wear an electric suit rather like an electric blanket, the purpose of which was to try and keep their bodies as warm as possible. On their heads they would have had a leather helmet which again would keep out the cold. Warm sheepskin gloves were worn to prevent frostbite. To take off the gloves at the high altitude would have meant instant frostbite and to touch a cold metal surface, such as their guns, would have meant they would have become stuck to them. Trying to operate the guns in the middle of a raging battle would have taken amazing physical strength and stamina. The crew would have to be extremely fit to take on flying duties.

Following Malcolm's death his body was buried at Madingley, Cambridgeshire, but later exhumed and returned to Lawton, Oklahoma for reburial July 16th 1948.

Malcolm's reburial at Lawton Oklahoma

Sgt. Maurice D Robbins, Tail Gunner

Maurice Robbins was born in Georgetown, Texas in 1923. He later moved to San Angelo, Texas, where he graduated from the San Angelo High School. On November 7th 1942 Maurice joined the Air Corps at San Antonio. He received his basic training at Miami Beach, Florida. Further training took place at the Aircraft Armoured School, Buckley Field, Denver, Colorado. From Denver Maurice travelled for continued tuition at the Gunnery School, Tyndoll Field, Panama City, Florida. While he was stationed at Tyndoll Field, Maurice was promoted to the rank of sergeant. Having received his new rank Maurice moved once again, for a short period of two weeks, to Salt Lake City, Utah, the U.S. home of the 305th Bomb Group.

Once again Maurice was stationed to another part of the U.S., Geiger Field, Washington. Here he finally met up with the crew that was to become *Mi Amigo*. The crew spent many hours flying together and preparing themselves for what was to come over the skies of Europe. The crew became a close knit team. Maurice became close friends with two of the crew in particular, fellow gunners Harry Estabrooks and Malcolm Williams.

As the tail gunner, Maurice's position was one of the most dangerous of all the crew. German fighters would attack the B-17s from the rear trying to take out the tail gunner before shooting at the engines. Statistically, more tail gunners were killed or wounded than the rest of the crew. The tail gunner would sit all alone beneath the huge tail with his twin .50 calibre machine guns. Crouched on a strange looking device that looked more like a saddle than a seat, searching the skies for a glint which might indicate approaching enemy fighters.

Following the crash of *Mi Amigo* in Endcliffe Park, Sheffield, Sgt. Maurice Robbins was buried at the American Military Cemetery, Madingley, Cambridgeshire. In attendance at the burial was Maurice's brother, Sgt. Raymond R. Robbins, a radio operator who was also a member of the 305th Bomb Group based at Chelveston, Northamptonshire.

The parents of Maurice Robbins received their son's posthumous medals, the Air Medal with oak leaf cluster and the Purple Heart. The citation which accompanied the medals read;

"For exceptionally meritorious achievement while participating in ten separate bomber missions over enemy occupied continental Europe. The courage, coolness and skill displayed by this enlisted man upon these occasions reflect great credit upon himself and the Armed Forces of the United States".

Crew Positions in Mi Amigo

Radio Compartment where Robert Mayfield would opera his radio plus man his single gun during attack. The gun was mounted in the per window that was a an emergency e

John Kriegshauser's seat. As pilot, John had the left seat and co-pilot, Lyle Curtis had the right seat. Harry Estabrooks manned the top turret during attack as well as assisting pilots in his other role as engineer.

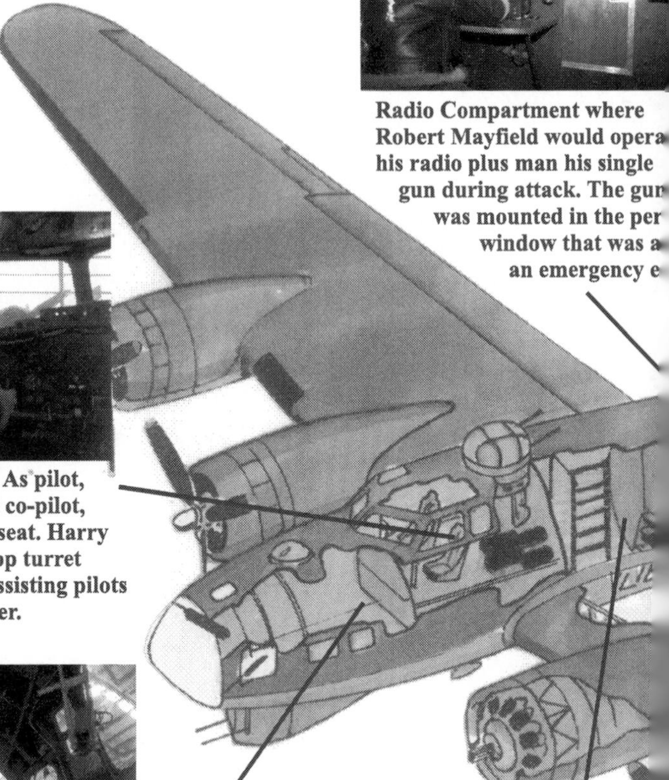

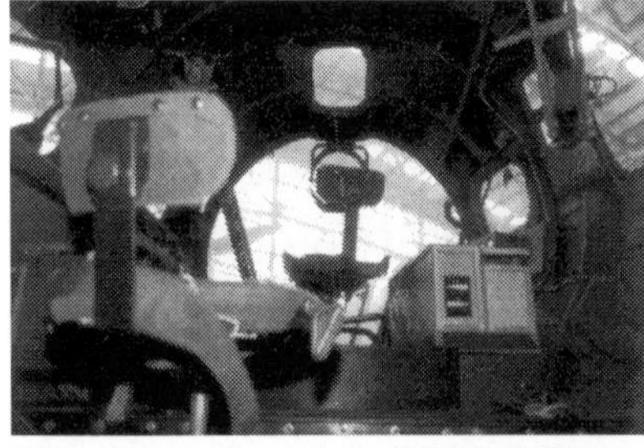

The nose section where Melchor Hernandez, the bomdardier, and John Humphrey, the navigator had their posts. During attack both men would use the two .50 calibre guns mounted either side of the nose as well as the remotely controlled chin turret for defence.

Bomb-bay, sho here complete 500lb bombs. C movement thro aircraft meant walking betwee bomb-racks. It a tight squeeze.

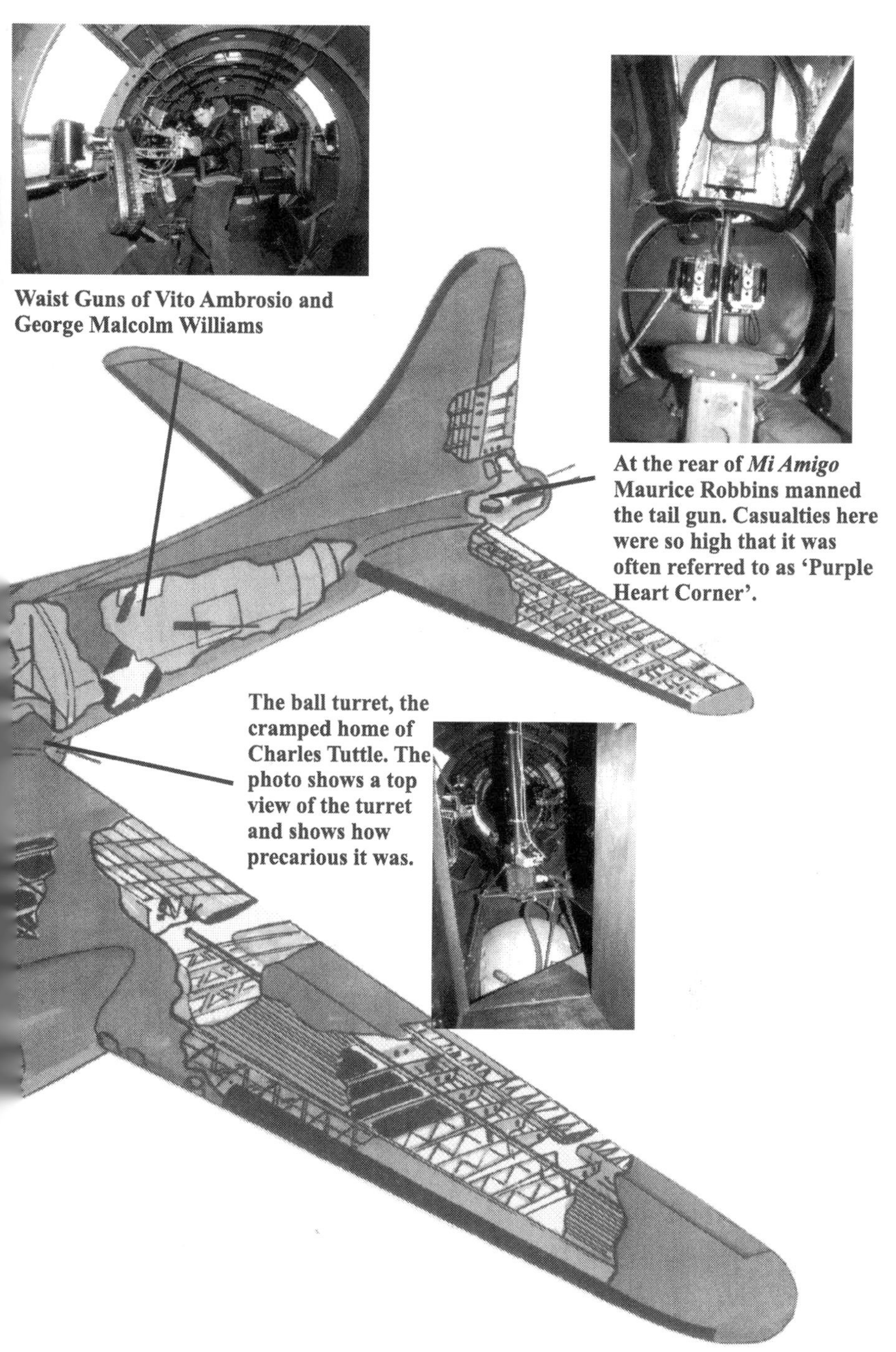

Waist Guns of Vito Ambrosio and George Malcolm Williams

At the rear of *Mi Amigo* Maurice Robbins manned the tail gun. Casualties here were so high that it was often referred to as 'Purple Heart Corner'.

The ball turret, the cramped home of Charles Tuttle. The photo shows a top view of the turret and shows how precarious it was.

The Final Mission

During the closing months of 1943, very serious consideration was being given by High Command to suspend all daylight bombing on Nazi Germany. The losses of crew and aircraft were unacceptably high. Morale was being severely affected, not just of the crews themselves, but also of the public in the U.S.A. It was vital to have long range fighter escorts for the bombers to and from the targets. The answer came in the form of the North American P-51D Mustang. This fighter had an outstanding performance and had the range to fly deep into Germany escorting the Flying Fortresses all the way.

P-51D Mustang

Allied High Command had been planning the invasion of Europe for some time. However, before D-Day and the eventual destruction of the Third Reich could be accomplished, it was realized that the Luftwaffe and its aircraft factories would need to be destroyed. It was therefore decided to step up daylight bombing and have a concerted effort to take out these facilities. The campaign became known as *Big Week.* Huge numbers of American bombers would fly en masse and destroy their aircraft related targets.

Early on the morning of February 22nd 1944, the crews from many bomb groups in eastern England were awakened for their briefing. There were various targets but, for the 305th Bomb Group, they were to take part in a diversionary raid on a Luftwaffe airfield, Alborg in northern Denmark. This airfield was known to be one of the most heavily defended in all of Nazi occupied Europe.

Alborg
DENMARK
GREAT
BRITAIN
Possible return route
Outward route of Mi Amigo
Sheffield
Chelveston
HOLLAND
GERMANY
FRANCE

The crews, having left the briefing room, collected their kit and were driven in jeeps and trucks to their waiting aircraft. The ground crews would have worked through the night making sure that the engines would perform to their maximum. Bombs and ammunition would have been loaded by the amourers and every last drop of aviation fuel would be loaded aboard the waiting B-17s. The morning of February 22nd 1944 was cold and damp with low cloud. As the crews waited for the order to take-off they would busy themselves with the pre-flight checks on navigation, instrumentation and radios.

Finally the order would have been given for engine start-up. The roar of dozens of Wright Cyclone engines would have reverberated across the airfield as the heavily laden B-17s slowly moved off their hard stands and onto the perimeter track, making their way towards the end of the runway, ready for take-off.

Lt. John Kriegshauser and his crew would have waited nervously at the end of the runway for their signal. Finally, a flashed Aldis lamp would have winked at them and the four mighty engines would have thundered up to full throttle. Every part of the aircraft would be vibrating. Every rivet, nut and bolt straining at the thin aluminum skin of the aircraft. Men praying that there wouldn't be an engine failure on take off. The brakes would be released from the wheels and *Mi Amigo* would have rolled down the runway for her last time. The speed would increase and the tail wheel would start to lift. Eventually, the aircraft would rise from the concrete runway, climbing up over the hedges and fields of the surrounding countryside. Climbing up through the cloud to join other aircraft from the 305th, the B-17s would form up over southern and eastern England.

To the people below it was a very familiar sight and sound. They had heard it almost every day for the last couple of years. As *Mi Amigo* moved into formation alongside other aircraft the weather was becoming worse. The temperature was falling and, more importantly visibility was deteriorating by the minute.

The Luftwaffe would have been tracking the approaching B-17s for some hours and, as *Mi Amigo* approached the Danish coast, the German defences would have alerted the anti-aircraft flak batteries and fighter squadrons of the attacking numbers of American bombers.

As *Mi Amigo* crossed the Danish coast, the American bombers were greeted by the all too familiar puffs of black smoke from the German flak batteries. Focke Wulf 190 fighters were also waiting for the approaching bombers and started their attacks almost immediately. The Flying Fortresses fought their way through the attacking swarm of fighters and continued on to their target, the airfield at Alborg. As they approached their objective, cloud completely obscured Alborg and, unable to locate the airfield, the aircraft turned for home with their bombload still intact.

The Focke Wulf 190s continued their attack on the formation of B-17s and *Mi Amigo* was singled out for attack. The crew fought back with their .50 calibre machine guns trying to ward off the ferocious attack. *Mi Amigo* was seen by other B-17s to take heavy damage, in particular to the engines. The bomb load was jettisoned over the North Sea in order to lighten the aircraft and to lessen the risk of explosion. *Mi Amigo* was now in serious trouble. With the loss of full power from her engines she started to fall behind the other bombers. It seems likely that the navigational instruments and radio were also badly damaged.

Another of the 305th's B-17s was also in trouble. Pursuing German fighters continued their attack until this second B-17 crashed into the sea off the Danish coast, killing all ten crew in the icy cold waters. *Mi Amigo* headed for England, not on a south westerly course towards Chelveston, but on a more westerly heading to Lincolnshire and Yorkshire beyond. It is for this reason that one assumes that navigation was proving difficult on board *Mi Amigo.* It may be that the navigator, Lt. John Humphrey, was either dead or badly injured. It may be that the pilot, Lt. John Kriegshauser, had badly injured crew aboard and he was trying to make the earliest landfall to enable the wounded to receive medical attention.

As the crew of *Mi Amigo* limped home to England they found that cloud obscured much of the ground beneath them. There were many airfields that *Mi Amigo* would have flown near to and it seems likely, therefore, that radio communications must have been knocked out. Otherwise, Lt. John Kriegshauser and his crew would have received directions to the nearest airfield. *Mi Amigo* approached the city of Sheffield and, as she flew low over the city, many people heard and saw the aircraft in a distressed state. Engines misfiring, firing and even sightings of flames trailing back from the wings. *Mi Amigo* flew on a straight course flying over Gleadless, Norton Lees, and Heeley. As *Mi Amigo* continued her low descent the crew appear to have spotted one of the few flat areas around Sheffield, Endcliffe Park.

It was clear to people on the ground that the American crew were looking for somewhere to land the stricken bomber. The N.F.S. [National Fire Service] were notified that a badly damaged aircraft was in danger of crashing on the highly populated city and units of the N.F.S. were despatched.

Lt. John Kriegshauser must have realised the extreme seriousness of the crew's dilemma. He started to circle the city in an effort to find a larger and safer place to land but, there were none. *Mi Amigo* flew so low over the roof tops that the local inhabitants could make out the faces of the crew. In the last dying seconds of *Mi Amigo's* flight, oil sprayed from the damaged engines covering the roofs around Endcliffe Park. Children playing football in the park saw the badly damaged Flying Fortress as John Kriegshauser and Lyle Curtis fought with the controls. Suddenly, one of the engines died and *Mi Amigo* plunged into the hillside of Endcliffe Park. The B-17 tore into the trees. The large tail section was ripped from the main fuselage, the wings folded and collapsed.

In an instant, fire broke out and ignited the remaining aviation fuel on board. The intense heat set off the .50 calibre bullets spraying the park with deadly pieces of steel. Civilians, soldiers and N.F.S. personnel raced across the park towards the burning inferno. The would-be rescuers had no idea whether bombs were on board the aircraft. Their only thought being to rescue the trapped crew inside. An unidentified member of the crew had been thrown from the aircraft when it had hit the ground. This crew member was carried away from the inferno but was found to be dead. One of the rescuers, Arthur Hayes, a decorator, found an axe that had been thrown clear of the aircraft and attempted to cut his way into the aircraft but was beaten back by the flames. A twelve year old boy, Arthur Needham, who had run into the park having seen the crash ran to the burning wreckage and found one of the crew still alive and trying to get out of the centre part of the burning fuselage. The airman cried out *"Can you save me kid ?"* Arthur noticed that the crewman was wearing a signet ring with the initial 'H' on it. Arthur tried pulling at the trapped airman's hand but was beaten back by the flames. He believed that the airman was trapped by his legs inside the wreckage.

Soldiers who arrived in the park threw a cordon around the park in an attempt to keep out onlookers. The concern of bombs on board was a very real threat. It took the N.F.S. over an hour to put out the flames.

Photographs of the smouldering wreckage graphically illustrate the extent of the damage

The tail section of Mi Amigo clearly displays the G in the triangle denoting the 305th Bomb Group

It was several hours before all the bodies were removed from *Mi Amigo.* John Kriegshauser and Lyle Curtis being the last to be removed. February 22nd 1944 was a black day for Sheffield, but it could have been much worse. In February 1944 Sheffield had a population of half a million. Sheffield had escaped a major disaster by a whisker. It was nothing short of a miracle.

Front page of
The Sheffield Telegraph
February 23rd 1944

nny INDEPENDENT—No. 27,850. FOUNDED 1819. 28, KIN[illegible] STREET. Tel. 26045 (ONLY ADDRESS)

Flying Fort Crashes In Sheffield Park

Bombs On London Again

AN alert was sounded in the London area last night.

Flares floated down in some areas, and high explosive and incendiary bombs were dropped.

Half-a-dozen raiders were pinpointed by dozens of searchlights at one time in various parts of the sky. An observer reported that hundreds of shell bursts were visible in the centre of each cone of searchlights as the guns attacked.

In one district the barrage was described as the heaviest of the war. For 15 minutes there was no cessation in the terrific bombardment, and houses shook from the reverberations. Fighters were working in close concert with the ground defences.

North Must Wait For Lemons

From Our Food Correspondent

Many parts of the North of England are likely to be the last to get supplies of lemons.

First cargoes reaching this country have already been distributed in Scotland, Cumberland and Westmorland. Further cargoes are [illegible] to London, the Southern [illegible] shire, but the rest of the North will have to wait for fresh shipments.

A Food Ministry official said yesterday that the lemons coming to Britain should be sufficient to supply approximately half a pound per head, or two to three lemons each.

They are not being rationed, and the Ministry appeals to retailers and consumers to see that distribution is fair.

Everyone His Own Coke Fetcher

Coke may now be acquired free [illegible] restriction or registration in [illegible] of not more than 56lb. [illegible] provided that the [illegible]uyer [illegible] himself.

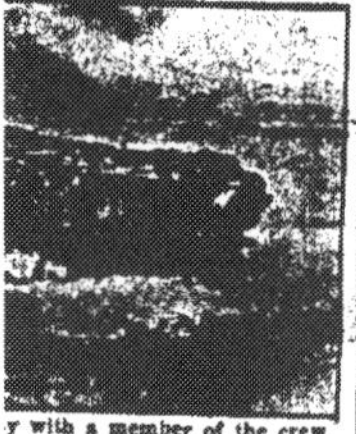

[illegible]y with a member of the crew [illegible] periscope.

[illegible] PUSH IS [illegible]T"—AXIS

[illegible]y Blitz Fails

[illegible]erman [illegible] Agency Cor[illegible] [illegible]t night that a big new [illegible]

CHILDREN in Endcliffe Park, Sheffield, escaped injury yesterday afternoon when a Flying Fortress crashed among the trees behind the refreshment bar and burst into flames. It is feared that the crew lost their lives. Trees were uprooted and crushed beneath the plane, and wreckage was scattered over the slope.

Mr. Will Griffiths, of Stainton Road, who was having tea when his wife told him the plane had crashed, ran out of the house in his slippers and, without a coat, waded across the brook and was the second to reach the bomber. A soldier was already there, and together they tried to make a hole in the metal sides with pieces of wood.

The front of the plane was blazing and the heat was too great for them to get near. Lying on the ground was one of the crew, whom they carried away from the fire, but they found he was dead.

Removed Ammunition

Arthur Hayes, of Bramall Lane, a decorator, who was working in a house near the park, heard the crash and ran out in his white coat. Finding a hatchet which had been thrown clear, he hacked a hole beside the rear turret. The gunner was not inside, but they removed the ammunition.

"I could hear the N.F.S. coming across the park," he said. "A few minutes later some soldiers came up too, and ordered all civilians away."

N.F.S. pumps poured water from the brook on the blazing wreckage, foam extinguishers were also used, and the pathways streamed with creamy foam.

Feared Bombs

Steel-helmeted N.F.S. men, C.D. workers, soldiers, and ambulance men helped to haul at ropes and remove the shattered wings so that rescuers could reach the remainder of the crew at the front of the bomber.

A cordon of soldiers was thrown around the park to keep away onlookers, for it was not known if there were bombs aboard the aircraft, and over an hour after the crash, flames still licked among the wreckage.

Part of the rear wing had been torn off by a branch of a tree 20 feet from the ground, several trees were uprooted and one was stuck in the middle of the plane.

A postman, Mr. William McNerlen, of 32, Stone Grove, Broomhill, who was delivering letters, saw the bomber spiralling downwards. "It rolled over three times and then crashed, and I rushed over to see if I could help as I am a first-aid man," he said.

"Victory" Roll

Among those who saw the plane immediately before its crash was Mrs. A. B. H. Clerke, of 14, Endcliffe Crescent, who was feeding the hens at the back of the house when she heard its engines.

"I waved to it, as I always do when I see a plane pass over," she said. "Then it came lower and gave what I thought must be a victory roll, and I was pleased to think the boys aboard had seen me wave and were answering.

"Suddenly the bomber made three terrific spins and plunged earthwards. It just cleared Endcliffe Grange, and was hidden from view behind the garden wall. A second later there was a terrible crash, a sudden uprush of flame, and I ran indoors to 'phone the police and N.F.S."

Two N.F.S. pumps, a salvage tender, and two foam units were rushed to the spot and over a score of firemen worked on the recovery of the bodies. Four hours afterwards the N.F.S. were still working in the light of acetylene flares.

RED ARMY 26 TO-DAY

STALIN HAILS ALLIED UNITY

HITLER'S Germany is on the road to catastrophe, but the Germans are still fiercely resisting and contesting every yard," Marshal Stalin said last night in an Order of the Day issued to the Red Army on the occasion of its 26th birthday to-day.

Reviewing the Russian victories, he added, "In the unfavourable conditions of the current winter our troops having overcome powerful enemy defence zones in three months of winter campaign have cleared the invaders from about 120,000 square miles of Soviet soil.

"If the Soviet Union, fighting single handed, was able to withstand the onslaught of the German Fascist armies, the plight of Hitlerite Germany will become still more hopeless when the main forces of our Allies enter the fray.

Sowing Discord

"The Fascist rulers are making desperate attempts to sow discord in the camp of the anti-Hitler Coalition and thus to protract the war.

"All these Hitlerite manœuvres are bound to fail, for at the basis of the anti-Hitler Coalition lie the vital interests of the Allies who have the task of defeating Hitlerite Germany and her accomplices.

"It is this community of fundamental interests which leads to the cementing of the fighting alliance between the U.S.S.R., Great Britain and the U.S.A."

Field - Marshal Sir Alan F. Brooke, Chief of the Imperial General Staff, has sent through the British Mission in Moscow a message to the Chief of Staff of the Red Army expressing his best wishes and personal greetings on the occasion.

LATE WIRES

BLACKOUT

To-day—7.00 p.m. to 7.38 a.m.

Moon rises 5.10 a.m., sets 5.45 p.m.

LONDON'S LONGEST THIS MONTH

All clear sounded. It was London's longest alert this month.

Faxon Man Gives Life For Others In England

The valiant crew of the Fortress Mi Amigo is pictured above. Bottom row, left to right, are Sgt. Maurice Robbins, tail gunner, Jonah, Tex.; S-Sgt. Raymond E. Mayfield, radio operator, Raymond, Ill.; S-Sgt. H. W. Estabrooks, engineer, Mound Valley, Kan.; Sgt. Vito R. Ambrosio, engineer, Brooklyn, N. Y.; Sgt. Charles H. Tuttle, ball turret gunner, Raceland, Ky., and M-Sgt. George M. Williams, waist gunner, son of Mr. and Mrs. George L. William, Faxon. Standing, left to right, are Lt. Melchor Hernandez, bombardier, Los Angeles, Cal.; Lt. J. W. Humphrey, navigator, Wyoming, Ill.; Lt. Lyle G. Curtis, co-pilot, Idaho Falls, Idaho, and Lt. John G. Kriegshauser, pilot, St. Louis, Mo.

The Lawton (Okla.) Constitution Monday Evening, December 25th 1944

After the Crash

Following the fatal crash of *Mi Amigo*, the cordon around Endcliffe Park continued for three days. During this time, the Army kept up their guard around the wreckage, ensuring that young boys and inquisitive adults did not try to take away souvenirs of the aircraft. An R.A.F. 'Queen Mary' recovery vehicle loaded up the wreckage that had once been *Mi Amigo* and transported it the U.S.A.A.F base at Abbotts Ripton in Cambridgeshire for disposal.

After three days the park was opened to the public. It is clear from eyewitnesses that the clear-up operation was far from thorough, although it must be remembered that snow covered the ground, hiding small fragments of metal from the B-17. However, larger more obvious items from the crash were found by intrigued members of the public. One eyewitness described finding a leather flying helmet and, on picking it up, discovered to their horror, part of a crewman's scalp still inside. Fragments of aluminum and Plexiglas from the windowed areas of the aircraft were taken as souvenirs. One newspaper reported that one of the seats was taken away by a group of boys. Many pieces of *Mi Amigo* were taken away. Sadly very few seem to exist today. One of the most interesting pieces of *Mi Amigo* to survive was given to me three years ago, a pair of airman's goggles. They were found by a young boy who came into Endcliffe Park when the park had just been reopened. Close to the cafe he noticed that something was glinting in the water. Curious, he waded in and pulled out a pair of goggles. To whom they belonged I do not know but, they are a salient reminder of that fateful day.

It is now fifty three years since *Mi Amigo* crashed in Endcliffe Park. Every year, a memorial service is held in the park at the crash site. The service is held on the Sunday closest to February 22nd. In 1969 Bert Cruse of the R.A.F.A. heard of the story of *Mi Amigo* and was sufficiently intrigued to attempt to research the crash. He believed, rightly, that a suitable memorial should be raised in memory of the ten young Americans who perished that cold February day in 1944. On November 30th 1969 a simple half ton piece of rough quarried stone was unveiled at the crash site. Two bronze plaques are attached to the stone. They read thus :

Erected by
Sheffield R.A.F. Association
In memory of
The ten crew of the U.S.A.A.F Bomber
Which crashed in this park
22-2-1944
Per Ardua Ad Astra

Air Crew

John G. Kriegshauser	Harry W. Estabrooks
Lyle J. Curtis	Charles H. Tuttle
John W. Humphrey	Maurice O. Robbins
Melchor Hernandez	Vito R. Ambrosio
Robert E. Mayfield	George M. Williams

At the unveiling ceremony were Major General John Bell, Commander of the 3rd U.S. Air Force, the Bishop of Sheffield, the Mayor and Mayoress of Sheffield and Bert Cruse.

In addition to the memorial stone, ten oak trees were planted close by, one for each crew member. The event was recorded by local T.V. and press. Many articles have appeared in the local press since the unveiling of the memorial stone. They usually appear in February to coincide with the anniversary.

Bert Cruse of the R.A.F.A. and Major General John Bell unveil the memorial stone in Endcliffe Park November 30th 1969

bove: Close-up of the plaques
ight: The Mayor of Sheffield
eaks to the assembled crowd

Fact, Myth and Legend

Not surprisingly, after a period of over fifty years, facts can often become hazy and distorted. *Mi Amigo* is no exception. The first example of this is that many people have believed for years that *Mi Amigo* was returning from Germany following a bombing raid. This is incorrect. It was known in 1963 that *Mi Amigo* had been returning from Denmark. It was reported in a lengthy article in The Star newspaper of September 4th 1969. Since this article, the facts of February 22nd 1944 have become lost in the mists of time.

In more recent years a new myth has emerged. The myth implies that *Mi Amigo* made a single long slow approach to Endcliffe Park. The purpose of which was to make a belly landing in the park. At the last moment it is said that the crew saw children playing in the park. The crew raised the nose of the aircraft avoiding the children, but hit the wooded hillside instead. This story has grown and has become part of the *Mi Amigo* legend. There is no factual evidence to support or corroborate this story.

The citation for Lt. John Kriegshauser's D.F.C. makes no reference to this version of the story. Newspaper reports from the day following the crash give several excellent first hand accounts, none of which use the story of the crew trying to avoid the children. The Star newspaper article from September 1963 which, to date has been the most accurate and lengthy, also makes no reference to *Mi Amigo's* crew trying to avoid the children.

This story appears to have started within the last seven years. I have spoken to many first hand witnesses and none of these support the myth. In fact a very different story emerges. When I first discovered that *Mi Amigo* had crashed in Endcliffe Park, I heard the story of the crew trying to avoid the children. I started to look for eyewitnesses to try and substantiate this. The story that I began to hear I found impossible to believe at first. I heard a description of the Flying Fortress falling, spinning from the low cloud that covered Sheffield that February afternoon. At first I dismissed this description. It was so at odds with the legend. I then heard the falling, spinning description a second and, again, a third time. By this time I couldn't ignore what I was hearing. I remembered something I had read from the front page of The Sheffield Telegraph of February 23rd 1944. It was the description given by a Mrs. A Clerke who lived on Endcliffe Crescent. She had been in her back garden feeding her chickens.

"I waved to it as I always do when I see a plane pass over. Then it came lower and gave what I thought must be a victory roll. Suddenly the bomber made three terrific spins and plunged earthwards. A second later there was a terrible crash"

This description is also confirmed in the same article by another eyewitness, William McNernlen, a postman.

"It rolled over three times and then crashed"

Late one night in November 1993, I received a telephone call from an eyewitness who had lived close to Endcliffe Park as a child and now lives in Florida, U.S.A. He had heard from a friend, who still lives in the Sheffield area, that I had been investigating *Mi Amigo*. He had been in the park on the afternoon of the crash. He had been playing snowballs with friends close to the cafe when, without warning, *Mi Amigo* fell out of the sky. His description made no mention of a long low approach for a belly landing.

In February 1994 I was in Endcliffe Park during the filming of the Yorkshire T.V. Edit V documentary. A man in his sixties was crossing the park and was clearly curious as to what was being filmed. When he realised that it was a documentary on *Mi Amigo* he described how, as a boy, he had seen the Flying Fortress. This eyewitness gave an extra clue as to what had probably happened. He graphically described how the crippled aircraft had been flying around the Ecclesall area for some time. The engine note suddenly changed and *Mi Amigo* fell out of the sky crashing into the trees below. I have spoken to B-17 experts about the change in the sound of the engines. They believe that one of two things happened. Either, the engines were starved of aviation fuel, or one of the engines suffered mechanical failure, possibly the result of enemy action. Either way *Mi Amigo* could not afford to lose power to any of its engines in what was already a crippled aircraft.

During the filming of Edit V Brian Pescud describes the end of Mi Amigo

During the filming of the Edit V documentary I spoke to another eyewitness, Brian Jackson. He too described the change in sound of the engines and saw it spin, crashing to the ground. Brian Jackson also described something that, up until that moment, I hadn't considered. The way in which the aircraft was positioned once it had hit the ground. I had heard the legend of *Mi Amigo* and the children so often and I had believed that the aircraft had approached Endcliffe Park from a southerly direction, ready to make its belly landing on the flat area of the park. If this were correct in that when *Mi Amigo's* crew had tried to avoid the children and impacted on the ground, the nose of the aircraft should have been pointing up the hill. Brian Jackson's description of the aircraft was that it was pointing down the hill, with the separated tail wedged firmly between the trees at the top of the hill. I checked my copies of photographs that were used in The Sheffield Telegraph and The Star from 1944. It was clear that Brian Jackson was correct. The photographs show the fall of the hill with the tail towards the summit. *Mi Amigo* had come from a northerly direction. It could not have been trying to make the infamous belly landing.

I have spoken to pilots who fly small single engined aircraft and they have all stated that they wouldn't even consider trying to land a small aircraft, never mind a four engined bomber there. From the air, Endcliffe Park looks nothing more than a tiny postage stamp.

It was reported in the local press some years ago that, a year after the crash in Endcliffe Park, another U.S.A.A.F. Flying Fortress flew low over the park and dropped a wreath to commemorate *Mi Amigo* and her gallant crew.

A strange twist to the tale of *Mi Amigo* has grown up around the immediate area of Endcliffe Park and is widely believed by many who live close by. It is thought that, on the anniversary of the crash, the ghosts of *Mi Amigo* wander through the park at night! I'm sure that the crew of *Mi Amigo* would be most amused at this imaginative notion. However, it clearly illustrates how myths and legends grow in the relatively short period of just fifty odd years.

Brian Jackson, eyewitness

Tony Kemplen

In January 1994 I heard of an artist named Tony Kemplen who was to have an exhibition of his work displayed at the Mappin Art Gallery in Sheffield. Tony's work was based on *Mi Amigo* and her crew. His exhibition was entitled SK329858 1944-94, derived from the ordnance survey map reference for the site of the crash and its anniversary. I telephoned Tony and suggested that we arrange to meet. He agreed and we met at the Mappin Art Gallery.

Tony was as anxious to meet me, as I was to meet him. We had both come under the spell of *Mi Amigo*. It was interesting that both Tony and I were from the south of England and were not from Sheffield as one might suppose. Tony explained that he was a mature art student studying fine art at Sheffield Hallam University. As part of his Fine Art degree course he had walked a route around Sheffield. The purpose of which was to find something local that would inspire him in his work. By chance, Tony came across the memorial stone in Endcliffe Park and was intrigued by the simple bronze plaques with the names of the ten crew of *Mi Amigo*. As he stood in the park gazing at the stone he became aware of the many aluminum ring pulls that littered the park. Tony was aware that the B-17 Flying Fortress was almost entirely made from aluminum. It occurred to him of the possible irony that, following the crash of *Mi Amigo* and the subsequent melting down of the wrecked aircraft, the ring pulls which littered the park *could* have been there once before in the guise of *Mi Amigo*.

Tony guided me around his exhibition which consisted of a series of ten prints, one for each crew member, collages, a series of playing cards depicting images of *Mi Amigo* and a 2ft square bronze relief of *Mi Amigo* flying over the area of Endcliffe Park. This last item is, for me, the centre piece of Tony's work relating to *Mi Amigo*. The influence of *Mi Amigo* is real, not just to me, but others too. Its lasting effect after fifty years is quite considerable.

When I first heard of Tony's exhibition, I have to admit that I was curious as to what the exhibition would consist of. I needn't have worried. Tony's excellent work expressed a real feeling for an event that happened so long ago. I hope that sometime in the future SK329858 1944-94 goes on public display again. It deserves another airing.

Tony Kemplen in front of part of SK329858 1944-94
and below some of his playing cards

Mi Amigo Today

For anyone wishing to look for evidence of *Mi Amigo* today, there are still items to be found in the way of memorials, buildings, graves and museums.

Memorial Stone

Endcliffe Park
Hunters Bar
Sheffield
South Yorkshire

Behind the cafe in the park is a stream which runs just below the hillside. Across the stream stands the memorial stone. It can be reached by using either the bridge to cross the stream or, alternatively, the large stepping stones provided.

Each year on the Sunday closest to February 22nd at the site of the memorial stone, a service is conducted by the Royal Air Force Association.

Memorial service on the event of the 50th anniversary of the crash February 22nd 19

The crash site today in conditions similar to those of the crash, January 1997

Endcliffe Park today. Mi Amigo crashed into the trees above right of the cafe

Airfield of the 305th Bomb Group

R.A.F. Chelveston
Off the A45
Chelveston
Nr Higham Ferrers
Northamptonshire

The airbase at Chelveston is still operated by the R.A.F. as a signals unit, but the airfield is no longer used for aircraft. The runways have long been torn up and used for hard-core for building motorways, etc. A single building stands on the former airfield, an enormous 'J' type hangar. It dominates the whole area. Originally the hangar was used to repair Flying Fortresses. In 1944 Major Glenn Miller and his Air Force Band gave a concert in this cavernous hangar. Today it is used by a local farmer for storing silage.

The desolate hangar is all that remains today of the 305th home base

Chelveston Church Tower

St. John the Baptist Church
Off the A45
Chelveston cum Caldecott
Nr Higham Ferrers
Northamptonshire

Within sight of the 'J' type hangar stands the ancient Norman church, St. John the Baptist. In the days when the 305th Bomb Group occupied the airbase at Chelveston, it was a welcoming sight to returning aircrews. In 1980 the 305th Bombardment Group [H] Memorial Association unveiled a memorial on the base of the tower, dedicated to more than 769 men killed and wounded during 480 separate missions.

Cambridge American Military Cemetery and Memorial

Coton
Cambridgeshire

The cemetery, more commonly known as Madingley, contains the remains of 3,812 American servicemen who were killed during World War Two. Amongst the white crosses lay the bodies of three of *Mi Amigo's* crew; Sgt. Charles H. Tuttle, Sgt. Harry W. Estabrooks, and Sgt. Maurice O. Robbins. Originally all of *Mi Amigo's* crew were buried here but, during the late 1940s, the families of Kriegshauser, Curtis, Humphrey, Hernandez, Mayfield, Ambrosio and Williams, requested the return of their sons, husbands and brothers for reburial in the United States.

Imperial War Museum

Duxford
Cambridgeshire

The former R.A.F. base at Duxford was, at one time, operating P-47 Thunderbolts and P-51D Mustangs operated by the U.S. 8th Air Force. It is now owned and operated by the Imperial War Museum and has one of the finest collections of World War Two aircraft in the world.

During the summer of 1997, a new hangar dedicated to American aircraft will open. Amongst the many aircraft is a B-17G named *Mary Alice.* This Flying Fortress is exceptional for its condition and is one of the best preserved examples of its type. It is a fitting tribute to all American aircrew who flew in the B-17 Flying Fortress. Many other artifacts relating to The U.S. 8th Air Force are contained within this new hangar.

P-47 Thunderbolt currently based at Duxford

Researching Mi Amigo

Researching an event that happened fifty years ago is not an easy task. Local newspapers are a good source of information and Sheffield newspapers during the war years, The Star and The Sheffield Telegraph, produced interesting reports. However, to write a book on *Mi Amigo* requires more than a few newspaper clippings. When I first discovered the crash in Endcliffe Park I recall reading the names of the American crewmen on the bronze plaque on the memorial stone. Thinking of the diverse origins of the surnames of the crew and of their home states back in America, it was clear that the crew were quite literally drawn from the length and breadth of the United States.

Trying to gain information on *Mi Amigo* has, at times, seemed almost impossible. There were occasions when I thought I may never get another new piece of data.

Unlike the R.A.F. the individual Bomb Groups of the U.S. 8th Air Force did not keep meticulous records of events. The priority was to bomb and destroy enemy targets. It was only towards the end of the war, when the end was within sight, that the various Bomb Groups started to document and record events for posterity. Unfortunately, many of the aircrews had been lost in action. Trying to piece together information about previous operations in any great detail, from the time when the Bomb Groups first arrived in England, proved almost impossible.

Here in Britain, the interest in the 8th Air Force is exceptionally high. One of the reasons for this is the series of books written by Roger Freeman who, as a boy, lived in East Anglia and marvelled at the skies filling with hundreds of American bombers and their fighter escorts. His books have become recognized as the foremost record of the 8th Air Force. However, even the books written by Roger Freeman give little mention of the crash in Endcliffe Park. This is no great surprise considering the thousands of aircraft lost by the 8th Air Force. On the day of February 22nd 1944, the 8th Air Force lost 43 bombers and 430 aircrew. It was not a good day for the *Mighty Eighth*.

I realised the best potential source of background information was the crew's next of kin and decided to track down the families. Bearing in mind the fifty years that had past, this was obviously going to be a difficult exercise. Many of the next of kin had died, leaving no known persons to contact. In many cases I managed to contact school friends who were a great source of information. In 1994, after twelve months of writing many letters, I was able to trace the widow and daughter of one of the crew. Mrs. Erma Thompson had been the wife of Lt Lyle J. Curtis, the co-pilot. Erma and her husband, Lyle, were married in the fall of 1943. They spent just six weeks together before Lyle was sent overseas. Their daughter Barbara was born in June 1944. Following the death of her husband Lyle, Erma remarried a few years later. The subject of her first husband, Lyle, was seldom mentioned in courtesy to her new husband Rao. In 1993, after many happy years of marriage, Rao died. It was only a short while later that I made contact with Erma. She and her daughter, Barbara, decided to visit England in May 1994. Neither Erma, or her daughter Barbara, knew much of the events of the crash and together we visited Endcliffe Park, Chelveston, Madingley and Duxford.

Barbara and her mother, Erma on their visit to the U.K.

Erma very generously gave me a close insight into Lyle, the events before he left for England and the time he spent at Chelveston. Barbara had never met her father.

"He had always been a photograph on the dresser"

During her visit to England she learnt much about her father. The brother of John Kriegshauser and sister of Malcolm Williams have contributed much to the background of their brothers and the lives they led back home.

A real hero

Widow salutes brave decision of WWII pilot

Dan Egan
Post Register

Erma Thompson learned of her young husband's war death 50 years ago this month.

"I found out on the fourth of March, 1944, with a telegram. They brought it to this house," Thompson said from her Idaho Falls residence last week. It took her longer to find out her husband died a hero.

The telegram only said 23-year-old 2nd Lt. Lyle Curtis died Feb. 22, 1944. It gave no details of his death — no explanation, no circumstances. It didn't say Curtis, a resident of Ucon, and the crew of his World War II bomber died so a group of children could live.

The 19-year-old widow had married her husband only six months earlier, while Curtis was on a 10-day leave. The two grew up together in the same eastern Idaho Mormon Church ward.

Within a few months of their marriage, Curtis, a pilot, received orders to go to Europe.

Because he was constantly on the move, the couple lived together for only six weeks. Home was a hotel in Spokane, Wash., where he was temporarily stationed.

"It was a precious time. I was so proud of him in his uniform. We'd walk down the street together and everybody would salute him," she said. "The only thing I was upset about was the fact that we had to live in a motel, so I couldn't cook for him."

He told her they would return to his grandfather's Ucon farm when the war ended, and raise horses.

Even though he was a co-pilot on a B-17 "Flying Fortress," flying dangerous missions over enemy territory, Thompson said she "was 100 percent certain" her husband would come home from the war unscathed. Still, that didn't make the day he left for Europe any easier.

"I don't think we said a whole lot to each other that morning, because he was upset and so was I," she said. It was November, and she didn't know she was pregnant.

She moved back into her parents' Idaho Falls home, and she and Curtis began writing to each other weekly. Most of his letters contained very little details of his life in England. The War Department censored some of what he wrote.

It was an anxious time for her.

"I was going to go to college. I didn't want to stay here and wait for his letters," she said. But she scrapped her college plans — with some disappointment — when she learned she was pregnant.

Curtis took the news of their pregnancy differently.

"He called it his 'blessed event,' "

See HERO, Page A3

Casualty of war

Photos by Robert Bower/Post Register and courtesy of Erma Thompson

Erma Thompson, below left, received the news of her husband's death in a terse telegram, above. It wasn't until months later that she learned Lyle Curtis, below right, died a hero. A bomber pilot in World War II, Curtis sacrificed himself and his crew to save a group of British children when he ditched his badly damaged plane in a forest rather than land on a playground.

Post Registrar - City of Idaho, USA on the 50th anniversary, February 1994

Tail Piece

Researching *Mi Amigo* has taken much longer than I ever expected. It has always been hard work, but always a labour of love. I have learnt a lot from *Mi Amigo* and her crew, more than just facts, figures and dates. I have met some excellent people, visited places far and wide and have had the opportunity to do some very interesting things as a result of my research. I always knew from the day I discovered *Mi Amigo* that there was a book waiting to be written. What I hadn't realised was that there were personal lessons to be learnt from the exercise.

Lt. John Kriegshauser was just twenty-three years old in 1944. He was in command of a U.S.A.A.F. Flying Fortress with a crew of ten. He always knew the risk to himself and the trust that his crew placed in him. Today, twenty-three seems a very young age to be in command of a crew of ten men, a heavy responsibility for a man of any age. Yet, Lt. John Kriegshauser carried his responsibility and position well. What is more, he never gave up on his men. He was determined to find somewhere to land his aircraft. He had fought his way back across the North Sea, trying to find somewhere to land his badly damaged aircraft and save the lives of his crew.

Whether *Mi Amigo* and her crew tried to avoid the children in the park, or not, is immaterial. What is important is that on a cold February afternoon in 1944, ten young American airmen, thousands of miles away from their homes, died whilst fighting a cause they believed to be right. They were not alone in their fight. Tens of thousands of allied airman also died during World War Two.

What makes *Mi Amigo* different is that it happened in a city park, here in Sheffield, my own back yard. I cannot think of any finer words to conclude this book, than those of Lt. John Kriegshauser himself. His last letter home to his parents says it all.

Adios, *Mi Amigo*.
David Harvey.
Dronfield Woodhouse, Sheffield. January 4th 1997.

Last Letter Home

Lt. John G Kriegshauser left a letter to be despatched to his parents should he fail to return.

"This is a letter I hope is never mailed. This letter isn't meant to be the final word from me, nor is it meant to build up false hope that I am still alive.

I am writing to let you know the various things that may take place. Should my ship be shot down, you would receive a telegram from the War Department, probably stating 'Your son has been reported missing in action'. This isn't the final word, but it does mean I've failed to return from a raid and as yet, no definite word can be given to you as to whether I've been killed or whether I've managed to get out of the ship.

If you should receive such a telegram, don't give me up as lost as it is very possible I am a prisoner of war, or that I've escaped capture and am escaping through France or possibly my ship was in such condition I was able to fly it over to some neutral country and am now interned in the country until the end of the war.

Should the final word come through 'killed in action', then there isn't much sense in having any false hopes because the telegram is the final word. If I am killed in action I want you, my folks, to know I couldn't have had better parents - parents who have constantly, throughout my span of life, done everything to make my life as full as humanly possible. I'm deeply grateful for every effort on your part and I'm sorry I didn't have the chance to repay you both in some small manner.

May God watch over you and protect you, and some day repay you for all the sacrifices you both made for me. As for Peg, I don't intend to write a letter of farewell but I do wish you would notify her of any telegrams you receive. Peg was the only girl I ever really loved and someday, as soon as possible, I had hopes of making her my wife.

My final word is that I'm glad to have been able to lay down my life for a cause which I believed was just and right".

Selected Bibliography

Bishop, Cliff	Fortresses of the Big Triangle First	East Anglia Books
Birdsall, Steve	B-17 Flying Fortress in color	Squadron/Signal
Birdsall, Steve & Freeman, Roger A	Claims to Fame, The Flying Fortress	Arms & Armour
Bowers, Peter M	50th Anniversary B-17 Flyng Fortress 1935-1985	Museum of Flight
Bowman, Martin W	Flying to Glory	P.S.L.
Bowman, Martin W	Four Miles High	P.S.L.
Campbell, John M & Donna	B-17 Flying Fortress Nose Art Gallery	Motorbooks Int.
Davis, Larry	B-17 In Action	Squadron /Signal
Ethell, Jeff	B-17 Flying Fortress	Motorbooks Int
Fox, George	8th Air Force Remembered	ISO
Freeman, Roger A	The Mighty Eighth	Arms & Armour
Freeman, Roger A	The Mighty Eighth War Manual	Arms & Armour
Freeman, Roger A	The Mighty Eighth War Diary	Arms & Armour
Freeman, Roger A	The Mighty Eighth In Colour	Arms & Armour
Freeman, Roger A	Airfields of the Eighth	After the Battle
Freeman, Roger A	B-17 Fortress at War	Ian Allan
Freeman, Roger A	B-17G Flying Fortress in World War Two	Ian Allan
Hess, William N	B-17 Flying Fortress	Motorbooks Int
Jablonski, Edward	Flying Fortress	Doubleday
Kaplan, Philip & Currie, Jack	Round the Clock	Cassell
Lande, D. A.	From Somewhere in England	Airlife
McDowell, Ernest R	Flying Fortress - The Boeing B-17	Squadron/Signal
O'Leary, Michael	B-17 Flying Fortress A Bombing Legend	Osprey Aerospace
Patterson, Dan & Perkins, Paul	The Lady	Ian Allan
Peeters, Willy	Boeing B-17G Flying Fortress	Verlinden
Thom, Walter W	The Brotherhood of Courage	305TH B.G.M.A.

Printed in Poland
by Amazon Fulfillment
Poland Sp. z o.o., Wrocław